BIO-TERRORISM

HOW TO TACKLE BIO-TERRORISM IN LONDON CITY

AUGUSTA KOROMA

Table of Contents

Figure

1: Showing a photo of Houses of Parliament UK. Source: (Westminister City Council 2014).

And a picture of Bioterrorism announcement. Source from (CDC, 2017)

Introduction

Westminster Borough Council Central London.

This is an interesting borough to explore with its vibrant locations and hierarchy in London. I love visiting this city and to focus on the needs of young adults and children.

After the devastating terrorist threats in Central London lately, it calls for an opportunity to implement change and work on improving the response rate at a certain level; to work on community resilient and more community engagement and readiness of bioterrorist attacks in central London.

The first thing that attracts visitors, tourist, and myself, or even members of the public is central London, wherein you can find hot spots areas like The Parliament, (Big Ben) West Minister Cathedral, Buckingham Palace, Hyde Park, Trafalgar Square.

I obviously thought these areas are the heart of London and to focus and conduct Health Need

Assessment (HNA) in the form of Bioterrorist threat in this community would be useful as part of public health intervention. It has been reported that Westminster Borough council has a larger population in London on businesses and visitor's attraction; as lots of people are in and out of the borough very quickly and out of the country (St Mungo's Broadway, 2015/2016).

Westminster city council is a borough in London that has been chosen to do this project because of recent theorist attacks in the city Public Health and crises are becoming increasingly complex as the demographics changes, the demand for public solution just increase; as lifestyle factors changes, the health challenges across the world place a higher demand on the public health sector with changes in the patterns of certain diseases and growing demand for advancement in medicine and technology.

As a result, the public health industry has never in the middle of a growing health crisis which are complex in nature. The connectivity of communities and increased migration has resulted in the easy migration or importation of health challenges that easily become epidemic and health care professionals are constantly, exploring ways to address the public health crisis confronting this century.

Westminster City Council consist of two parliamentary areas which includes Westminster North: Members of Parliament Karen Buck from the labour party; focusing on these constituency: Bayswater, Abbey Road, Harrow Road, Church Street, Lancaster Gate, Queen's Park, Little Venice, Regent Park, and Westbourne. London and Westminster Cities: Members of Parliament Mark Field's from the conservative party local areas are: Knightsbridge, Bryanston, Dorset Square, Churchill, Belgravia, Marylebone High Street, Tach brook, St James's, Vincent Square, West End, and Warwick (City of Westminster Council committees 2017).

The West Minister Council Joint Health and Wellbeing consist of central, West London, West Minister City Council, National Health Services (NHS), Clinical Commissioning groups, Voluntary groups, the community, Health Sector care givers, with a vision of great wellbeing enablement of the population in West Minister and to be health in collaboration of joint working health care provision (Joint Health and Wellbeing Strategy for West Minister 2017-2020).

Existing Community Health Needs Assessment (HNA)

The focus on Public Health involves wellbeing, prevention, health promotion. However, Baggott (2011), stated that Public Health deals with the durability of the population and to the extension of free ill health in a community. The Local Government and Public Involvement in Health Act Section 116 places an obligation on the local authority to undertake a JSNA (AHMSO, 2007) and the Westminster Council regularly carry out their assessment to ensure the health and wellbeing of their local population; this is stipulated in their Joint

Health and Wellbeing Strategy 2017-2022 (Westminster City Council, 2017).

The previous HNA is called Joint Strategy Needs Assessments (JSNA) 2012, 2013-2014, 2015-2016 with an existing funding of 2,638,491 in 2016 to 2017 which consist of three boroughs including Westminster, Hammersmith & Fulham, Kensington, and Chelsea (Joint Need Assessment, 2016). The Joint Health and Wellbeing Strategy (JHWS) 2017-2022 is the current HNA which would have established the target of this project.

Identifying Health Needs Assessment Analysis

To identify health needs assessment, Community Health Needs Assessment (CHNA) main strategy is to execute a master plan to strategically reposition the importance of health reform in the population (Joint Health and Wellbeing Strategy for Westminister 2017). However, Rowe, McClelland, Billingham, (2010) described Community Health Needs Assessment as a procedure which:

- characterises the community of health for people that are living in a local area.

- Provide the means of surveillance of the main risk problems and instigates ill health.

- Provide the classification of the activities needed to follow the issues as it is a progressive process.

The North-West London sustainability and Transformation Plan (STP) consist of eight Clinical Commissioning which includes Westminster. Key Strategies focus are:

- Better outcomes for Children and young individuals in health management.
- Cutting down on health risk management

- Leadership in Mental Health well-being.
- Sustainability Care for local Community and the Care approach for Westminster. However, in a nut shell the service delivery is done by focusing on the quality of people's lives, experiences with a key target on the financial upkeeping of care provisions and health care (Healthier North-West London, 2016).

An example of these needs is illustrated below.

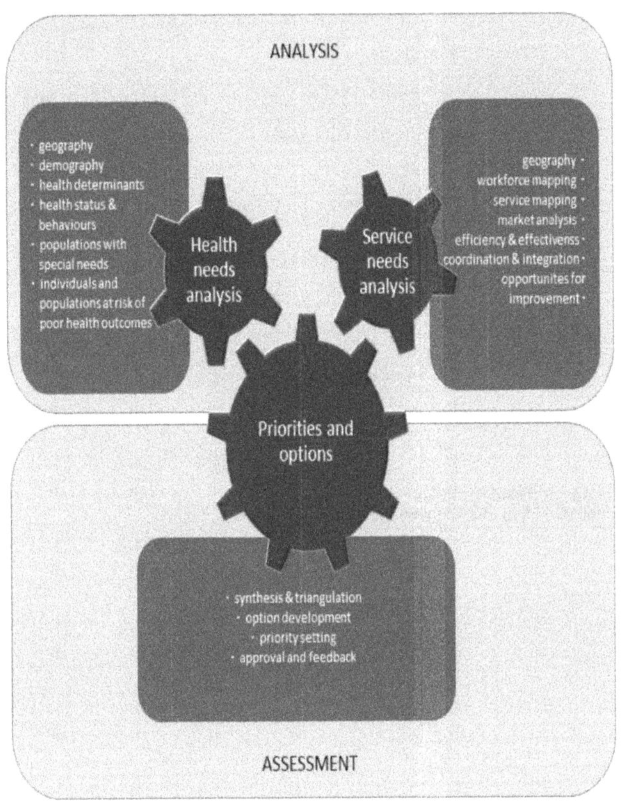

Figure 2: According to the Australian Government Department of Health, (2015) this structure analysis should be the key focus on Community Needs Assessment.

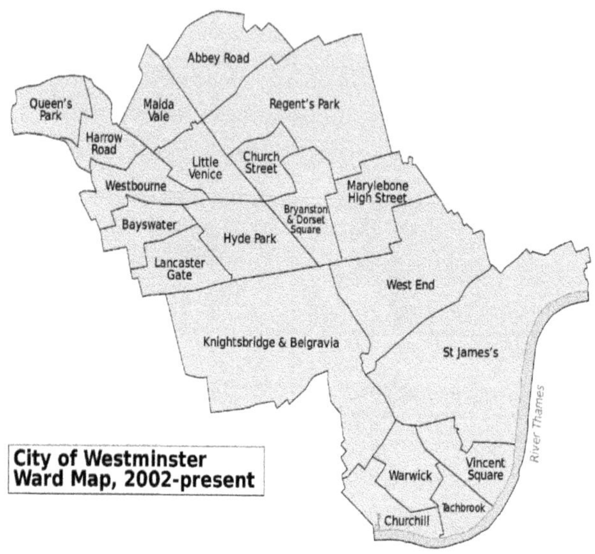

Geographical Location of Westminster council

Figure 3: Showing the city of Westminster borough council. Derived from Westminster London UK labelled ward map SVG (2002).

A further analysis of the Westminster Council is necessary considering the push factor that attracts visitors to the area from all over the world and the possibility of bioterrorism is visible if appropriate measures are not in place. Using a cause and effect diagram, the author illustrates the different health challenges that could emerge from bio-agent attack

DEMOGRAPHIC

POPULATION AND MIGRATION

Westminster City Council has been classified as a global community with a population of 233,900 people; with prediction to rise at 257,418 in the year 2040, a day time estimated amount of 1.1 million people as the top day time population which results in inhabitants, visitors, and employees in London (ONS MYE 2014).

According to the city of Westminster Economic Report LEA Baseline Study, (2016) the Council has a wide varying ethnic residents of differential health needs; people who are not born in the United Kingdom (UK) resides in West minister of a significant amount of 219,396 at 53% and consist of the third highest local authorities in the U.K (Census, 2011). Conversely, the population has increased with migration. Here is a graph showing the 2017 up-to-date population and Migration:

Figure 5: Showing Westminster Migration Trends. Source Census, 2011.

TOURISM

Westminster attract over 55 million visitors a year, with tourism expenditure totalling nearly £7bn according to LDA, 2007. The borough is home to 5 of the tope 20 paid attractions in London and 6 of top 20 unpaid attractions with 450 hotels providing 40% of all London's bed spaces, with numerous international high-end hotels alongside other accommodation types (Westminster City Council, 2014).

As a result, the City of Westminster is a magnet to many tourists visiting the United Kingdom visiting the House of Parliament, Westminster Abbey, Horse Guard etc.

Figure 6: Showing an outlook of the Houses of Parliament. Source Westminster City Council 2014.

AGE STRUCTURE

According to the city of Westminster Economic Report LEA Baseline Study, (2016) the population comprises of young adults with a figure of 23% of the community are aged ranging from 25-34 with majority are women of aged 55 and above; lesser number of children and older generation in the city compared to London and the UK. Elderly over 65 are fully engaged in terms of culture, economically, socially active and into the workforce in terms of volunteering role, caring for children and grandchildren, civil workers and health professionals

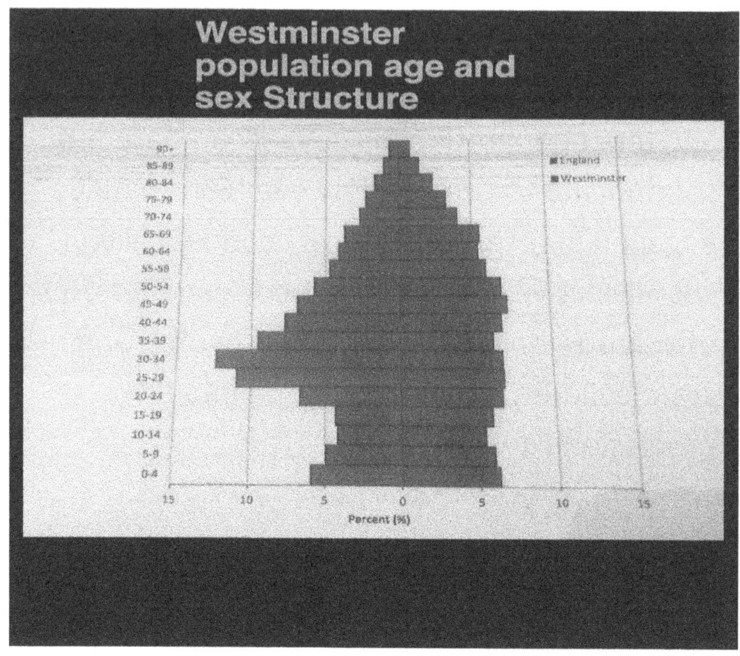

Figure 7: Showing the Population age and Sex Structure of Westminster City Council compared to England. Source:Westminister Council LEA Baseline Sturdy 2016).

Gender Classification

When it comes to gender specification in West minister city council, there were more females than males residing in the community. Here is a chart showing age structure for five years age group and gender in the year 2013. As stated by ONS, (2014) this has changed in 2017, there are more males living in the community than females.

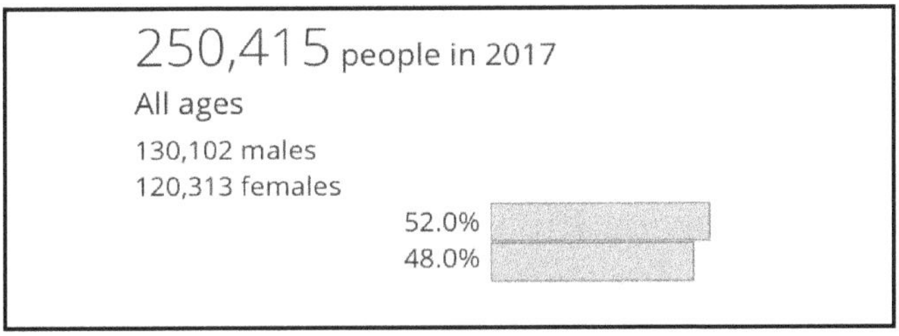

250,415 people in 2017
All ages
130,102 males
120,313 females
52.0%
48.0%

Figure 8: Showing the present Gender for Westminster Council. Source, ONS, (2014).

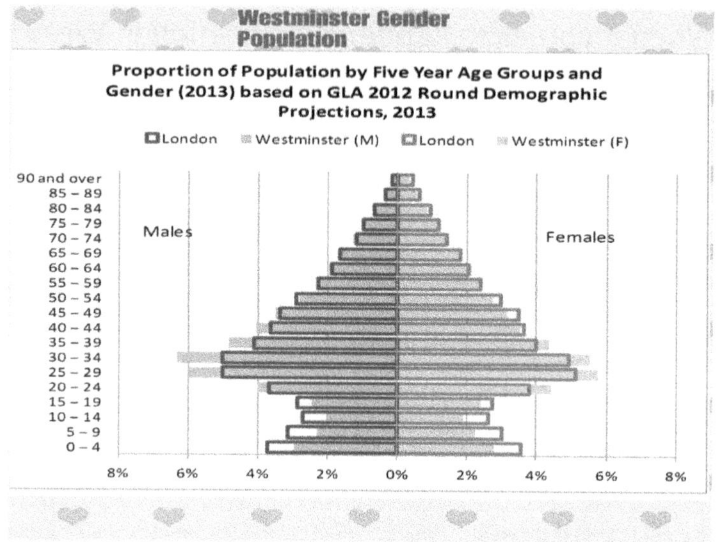

Figure 9: Showing the gender Population of West Minister City Council. Source: (Westminster Profile, 2014).

•

Ethnicity/ Nationality Communities

According to the Simpson Diversity score index below (ONS, 2012) Westminster City Council has the highest diverse Community in London ranged at 9 in London including 10 of local 455 communities in England and Wales.

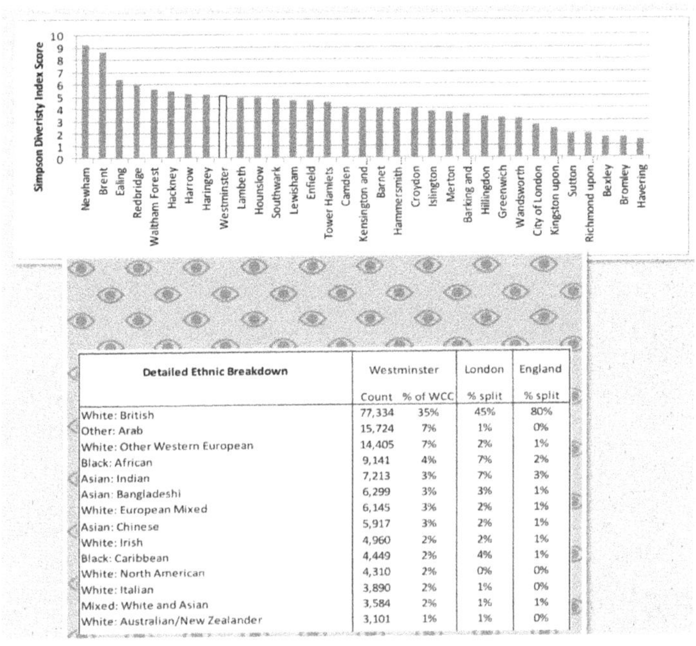

Detailed Ethnic Breakdown	Westminster		London	England
	Count	% of WCC	% split	% split
White: British	77,334	35%	45%	80%
Other: Arab	15,724	7%	1%	0%
White: Other Western European	14,405	7%	2%	1%
Black: African	9,141	4%	7%	2%
Asian: Indian	7,213	3%	7%	3%
Asian: Bangladeshi	6,299	3%	3%	1%
White: European Mixed	6,145	3%	2%	1%
Asian: Chinese	5,917	3%	2%	1%
White: Irish	4,960	2%	2%	1%
Black: Caribbean	4,449	2%	4%	1%
White: North American	4,310	2%	0%	0%
White: Italian	3,890	2%	1%	0%
Mixed: White and Asian	3,584	2%	1%	1%
White: Australian/New Zealander	3,101	1%	1%	0%

Figure 10: Showing Diversity score index and ethnic breakdown of diverse communities in

Westminster City Council compared to London and England. Source: (Census, 2011)

Beliefs or Religion

Westminster council present to have a higher number of Christians as listed below:

Religion	Total (in thousands	%
Christian	97.8	45%
Buddhist	3.2	1.5%
Hindu	4.2	1.9%
Jewish	7.2	3.3%
Muslim	40.1	18%
Sikh	0.5	0.2%
Other religion	1.3	0.6%
No religion	44.5	20%
No religion stated	20.5	0.1%

Figure 11: Showing Religious trends in Westminster City Council. Source derived from Westminster City Council (2013).

Community Safety and Transportation

It has been proposed that Westminster City Council has the most crime rates on theft and handling mainly because, of tourist attraction; approximately 26,000 reported crimes from the year 2015 to 2016. Violation on person is the second one resulting on 9,500 reported cases in the year 2015-2016. The graph below we give a great insight into reported crimes.9

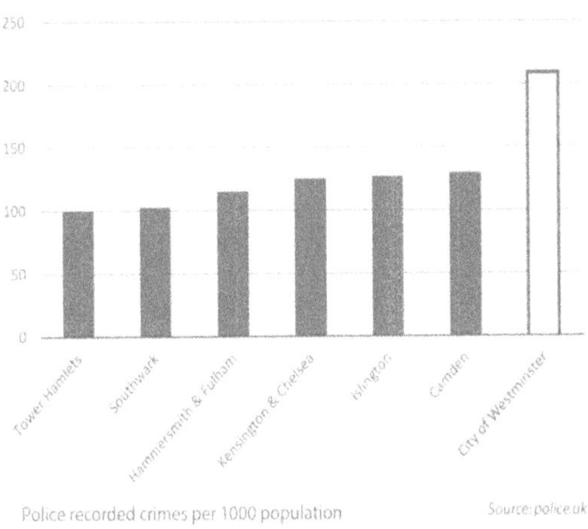

Figure 13. Showing crime rate of London's borough council. Source: Metropolitan Police, (2017).

To be accurate, Westminster City Council most favourite strength in the economy is access and connection around greater London and various areas in the south east; with 32 stations in the council on transportations and 10 of the total 12 via underground and four main point of rail stations including 80 bus routes and four piers river boat commuters' provisions.

The council has four in total of the ten active London underground stations in London which includes Oxford Circus, Victoria, Piccadilly Circus and Paddington with the largest of them all is Victoria station with 87 million passengers yearly; and overall passengers yearly in Westminster is approximately over 667 million as in 2012 (Westminster city Council 2016).

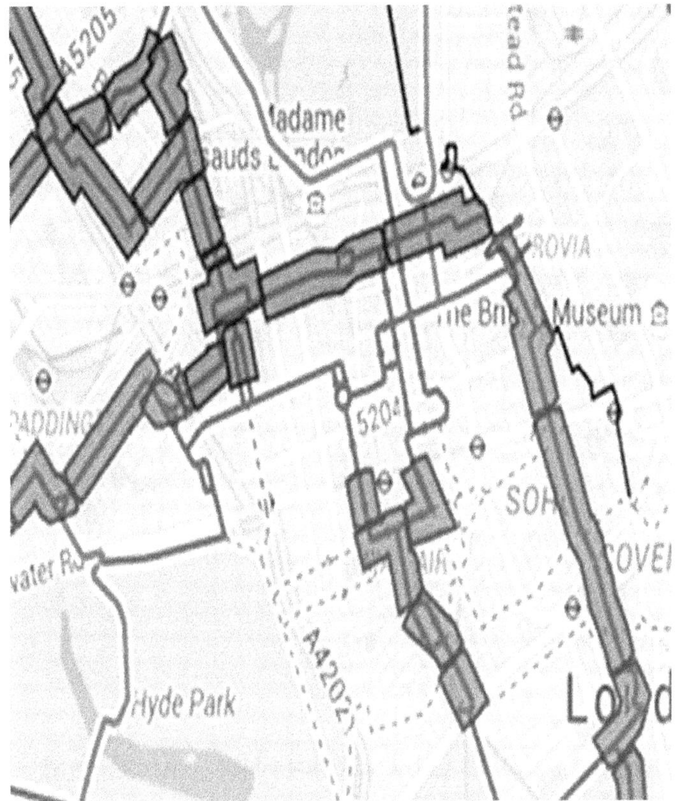

This Photo by Unknown Author is licensed under CC BY-NC-SA

Figure 14. Showing Westminster major transportation Rail stations. Source: google

Westminster City Council, (2015) stresses the need for socio economic and environmental issues that it cannot be done alone and needs collaborative partnership with the public involvement interventions, businesses, communities. For example, Community integration in Neighbourhood watch.

Health inequalities

According to ONS (2015) takes the stance that Westminster is a place with both ends of richest and has the higher rate of deprived areas Index Multiple Deprivation (2015) has conducted a surveillance and it is reported to be 57th deprived including other areas in England districts. Here are few facts listed below:

Domain	Domain weight (%)
Income Deprivation	22.5
Employment Deprivation	22.5
Health Deprivation and Disability	13.5
Education, Skills and Training Deprivation	13.5
Barriers to Housing and Services	9.3
Crime	9.3
Living Environment Deprivation	9.3

figure 10: Showing 2015 Index Deprivation in Domain and weight

Source: Index of Multiple Deprivation (2015).

Health Summary

Public Health England, (2016) states that Westminster city council is 20% deprived population amongst various other district, and children are 30% which is about (8,300) are staying in low income families; as life expectancy in female and male are quite higher compared the England average population.

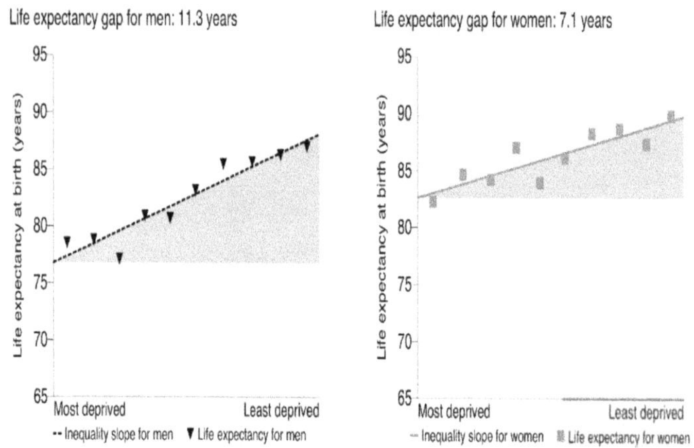

Figure 11: Showing Life expectancy for men and women.

SOCIO-ECONOMIC, CULTURAL ENVIRONMENT STRUCTURES

The cultural, economic, and social structure of Westminster based on space is a huge factor on the environment and more restriction on space in the environment which poses great demand on housing problems; most residents are on rental lettings in both private and public provisions which creates more housing cost leading to deprivation of poverty compared to other people in their own homes (Westminster Council 2014). Dahlgren and Whitehead (1991) takes the stance that to be

effective, various policies need to be lower in health inequalities should be handle in all areas of the issues which includes environment, socio-economic problems, living conditions, individual lifestyle factors, community influences, and working conditions. These are as follows:

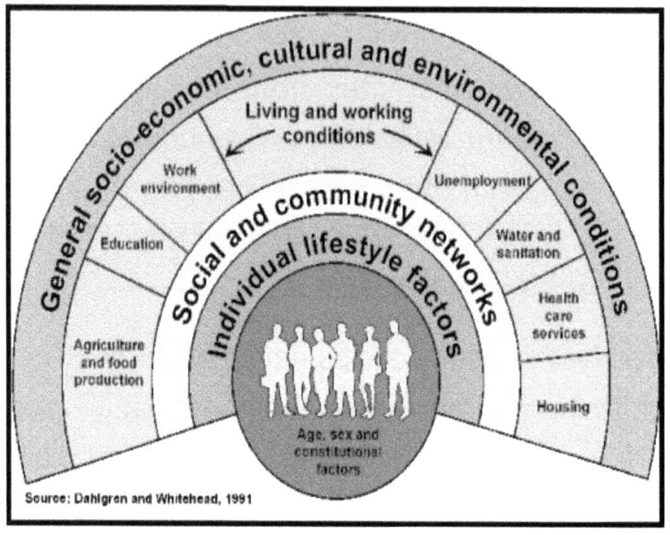

This Photo by Unknown Author is licensed under CC BY-NC-ND

Figure 12. showing the rain bow model of health. Source: (Dahlgren &Whitehead 1991).

Cultural

Westminister Council has the most diverse community in the country with all different nationalities.

Economy

When it comes to economic activities in London, Westminster city council has the lowest economical active inhabitants, approximately 69.9% of the population working age are very active as it is quite low in comparing to London with an average of 77.4%.

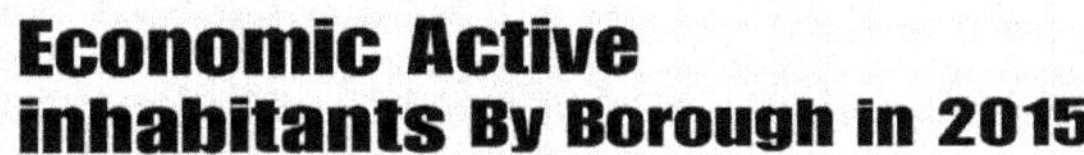

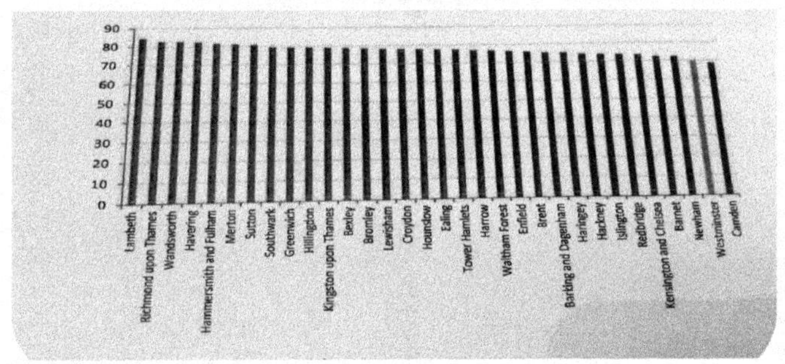

Figure 14. Showing the economic active inhabitants by various borough in London.

Source: (LEA Baseline Study Westminister Council 2016)

Unemployment and Mental Well being

It has been proposed by Annual Population survey (2015) that unemployment rate in Westminster city council has been alternate from the year 2007 and varies around the year 2008 to winter 2010 as unemployment goes up during the seasons of winter than summer. Here is a graph below explaining the insight of unemployment and job seekers claimant rate from the year 2008 to 2015.

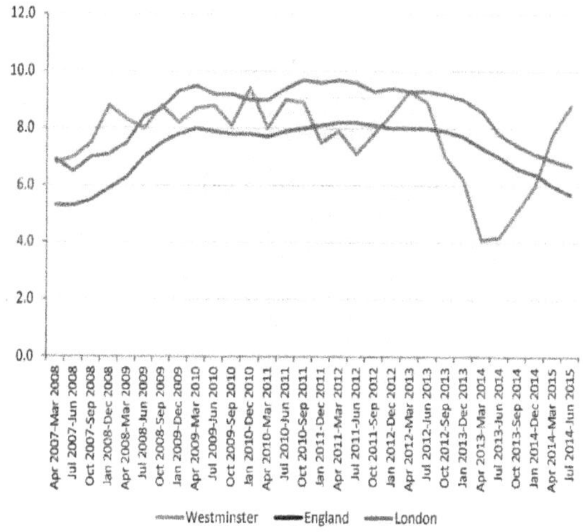
12.0
10.0
8.0
6.0
4.0
2.0
0.0
Apr 2007-Mar 2008
Jul 2007-Jun 2008
Oct 2007-Sep 2008
Jan 2008-Dec 2008
Apr 2008-Mar 2009
Jul 2008-Jun 2009
Oct 2008-Sep 2009
Jan 2009-Dec 2009
Apr 2009-Mar 2010
Jul 2009-Jun 2010
Oct 2009-Sep 2010
Jan 2010-Dec 2010
Apr 2010-Mar 2011
Jul 2010-Jun 2011
Oct 2010-Sep 2011
Jan 2011-Dec 2011
Apr 2011-Mar 2012
Jul 2011-Jun 2012
Oct 2011-Sep 2012
Jan 2012-Dec 2012
Apr 2012-Mar 2013
Jul 2012-Jun 2013
Oct 2012-Sep 2013
Jan 2013-Dec 2013
Apr 2013-Mar 2014
Jul 2013-Jun 2014
Oct 2013-Sep 2014
Jan 2014-Dec 2014
Apr 2014-Mar 2015
Jul 2014-Jun 2015
Westminster
England
London

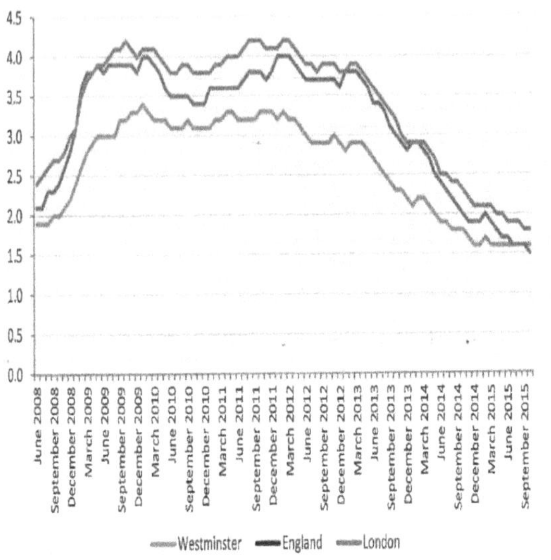

Figure13: Showing graphs of unemployment jobseekers for Westminster city council

Work Environment Access

One of the main vision of West minister council is to generate possibilities in helping people to work around the city and by gaining greater access to employers in a diverse workforce (Davis, 2017). It has been suggested that Westminster City Council demands and needs of their population should be changed to a workforce in training individually despite of ill-health into a better strategy and well packed to work collaboratively in the community to avoid ill health; investment in training nurses and other health care professionals to work on person centred care holistically in the community, improve better infrastructure management in Crossrail, which will create a larger workforce so that people can commute to the city easily (Westminster City Council, 2015).

SOCIAL AND COMMUNITY NETWORKS

Restoration

Westminster Council has approximately 40% of guest houses and hotels in London with highlight of tourist attractions such as Houses of Parliament, Buckingham Palace, Westminster Abbey, London Zoo, National Gallery, National Portrait Gallery, and Tate Britain.

According to The Public Health England (2016) main areas of public health concerns in Westminster City Council are as follows:

- Bioterrorism in biological weapon on Anthrax
- Small Pox
- Measles
- Cholera
- Food safety- E-Coli
- Ebola Virus

Westminster priority areas include reduction of obesity in children, lowering of smoking in the community, improving sexual health, mental health, substance misuse, better services and creating better employment. Although all these have been raised as a public health concern, the need for Bioterrorist threat calls for preparedness in the community as listed above(Public Health England 2016).

COMMUNITY HEALTH NEEDS ON BIOTERRORISM HEALTH PRIORITES AND INTERVENTIONS

<u>Identifying Community Health needs and interventions in Bioterrorism.</u>

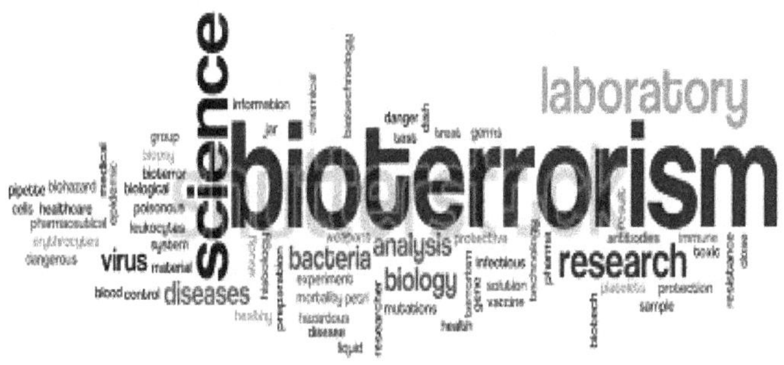

According to Pal et al, (2017), Bioterrorism is the act of preconceived, scare, use of pathological Factors; various viruses, poisons, pathogens, or few lists of other executors creating ill health in people, plant, or animals.There are various forms of biological Bioterrorism agents such as Anthrax, cholera, Ebola, and food safety in Salmonella. .

According to Nsubuga, (2017) there has been few terrorist attacks in the Westminster Council area including Buckingham Palace, London Bridge, and Parson Green. Farmer, 2017 reported that Bill Gates called for a warning on Bioterrorism in a global world and frequent methods in genetic measures have created few terrorisms emerges could relate to biological agents into mass destruction in chemical weapons and that public health agencies should be looking at defending bioterrorism and be ready to tackle the epidemic when it comes.

However, because of the growing concerns, bioterrorism in terms of chemical destruction could be looked at and the readiness of the Public Health sector to handle evolving bioterrorist threat in central London; is a way of focusing on the community and the public in relation to public health. Also following the incident that took place in London on July 5th2005, biological chemicals were found in five patients bodies which seems to be gathered from soft tissues in hospitals (Thompson et al; 2014).

Westminster has a vast challenge mainly because it is situated at the central part of London. However, it is stated by Westminster City Council (2015) that it has the largest population of people sleeping in the streets and that alone can count on mental, physical health issues if it is compared to the rest of the overall population with a great proportion of alcohol misuse; causing huge pressure to the NHS as they attend accident and emergency services seven times higher than the rest of the population.

If ever there is a bioterrorist attack in Central London, it will create a whole lot of catastrophe with these rough sleepers in the community. Pal et al, (2017) expresses that is deadly and has the potential of killing lots of people in the space of a short time; Bioterrorism has a great impact in high mortality rate and morbidity, in terms of aerosolised biological weapon.

According to CDC (2017) these are some of the main crucial agents of bioterrorism are as follows including history of outbreak below:

Disease	**Pathogen**	**Used**
Group A (High Priority public health hazards)		
Anthrax	Bacillus anthracis	World War I; World War II; Soviet Union, 1979; Japan, 1995; USA, 2001
Botulism	Clostridium botulinum	–
Haemorrhagic	Marburg virus	Soviet bioweapons programme
Fever	Ebola virus	–
	Arenaviruses	–
Plague	Yersinia pestis	Fourteenth-century Europe; World War II
Smallpox	Variola major	Eighteenth-century North America
Tularaemia	Francisella tularensis	World War II

Group B (public health hazards)		
⍰ Encephalitis	Alphaviruses	World War II
⍰ Food poisoning	Salmonella species, Shigella species	World War II; USA, 1990s
⍰ Glanders	Burkholderia mallei	World War I; World War II
⍰ Psittacosis	Chlamydia psittaci	–
⍰ Q-fever	Coxiella burnetti	–
⍰ Typhus	Rickettsia prowazekii	World War II
⍰ Various toxic syndromes	Various bacteria	World War II

Figure 17: Showing various Bioterrorism threats diseases, pathogens, and used. Source, (Barrasa, Greubb, 2014).

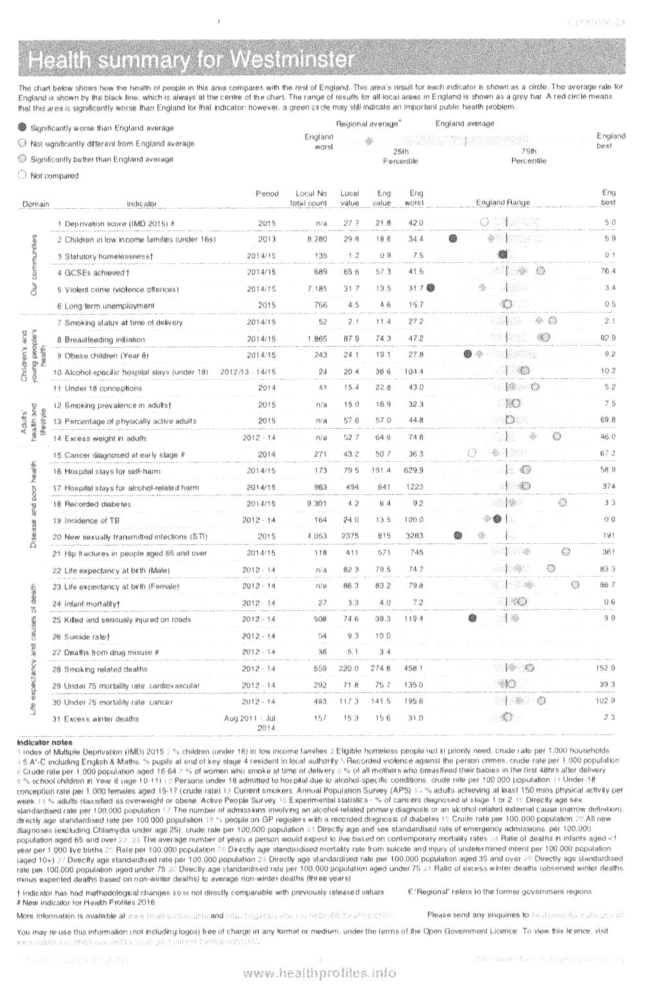

Health summary for Westminster

The chart below shows how the health of people in this area compares with the rest of England. This area's result for each indicator is shown as a circle. The average rate for England is shown by the black line, which is always at the centre of the chart. The range of results for all local areas in England is shown as a grey bar. A red circle means that this area is significantly worse than England for that indicator; however, a green circle may still indicate an important public health problem.

Domain	Indicator	Period	Local No total count	Local value	Eng value	Eng worst	England Range	Eng best
Our communities	1 Deprivation score (IMD 2015) #	2015	n/a	27.7	21.8	42.0		5.0
	2 Children in low income families (under 16s)	2013	8,280	29.8	18.6	34.4		5.9
	3 Statutory homelessness†	2014/15	135	1.2	0.9	7.5		0.1
	4 GCSEs achieved†	2014/15	689	65.6	57.3	41.5		76.4
	5 Violent crime (violence offences)	2014/15	7,185	31.7	13.5	31.7		3.4
	6 Long term unemployment	2015	756	4.5	4.6	15.7		0.5
Children's and young people's health	7 Smoking status at time of delivery	2014/15	52	2.1	11.4	27.2		2.1
	8 Breastfeeding initiation	2014/15	1,865	87.9	74.3	47.2		92.9
	9 Obese children (Year 6)	2014/15	243	24.1	19.1	27.8		9.2
	10 Alcohol-specific hospital stays (under 18)	2012/13 - 14/15	24	20.4	36.6	104.4		10.2
	11 Under 18 conceptions	2014	41	15.4	22.8	43.0		5.2
Adults' health and lifestyle	12 Smoking prevalence in adults†	2015	n/a	15.0	16.9	32.3		7.5
	13 Percentage of physically active adults	2015	n/a	57.6	57.0	44.8		69.8
	14 Excess weight in adults	2012 - 14	n/a	52.7	64.6	74.8		46.0
Disease and poor health	15 Cancer diagnosed at early stage #	2014	271	43.2	50.7	36.3		67.2
	16 Hospital stays for self-harm	2014/15	173	79.5	191.4	629.9		58.9
	17 Hospital stays for alcohol-related harm	2014/15	963	494	641	1223		374
	18 Recorded diabetes	2014/15	9,301	4.2	6.4	9.2		3.3
	19 Incidence of TB	2012 - 14	164	24.0	13.5	100.0		0.0
	20 New sexually transmitted infections (STI)	2015	4,053	2375	815	3263		191
	21 Hip fractures in people aged 65 and over	2014/15	118	411	571	745		361
Life expectancy and causes of death	22 Life expectancy at birth (Male)	2012 - 14	n/a	82.3	79.5	74.7		83.3
	23 Life expectancy at birth (Female)	2012 - 14	n/a	86.3	83.2	79.8		86.7
	24 Infant mortality†	2012 - 14	27	3.3	4.0	7.2		0.6
	25 Killed and seriously injured on roads	2012 - 14	508	74.6	39.3	119.4		9.9
	26 Suicide rate†	2012 - 14	54	9.3	10.0			
	27 Deaths from drug misuse #	2012 - 14	36	5.1	3.4			
	28 Smoking related deaths	2012 - 14	559	220.0	274.8	458.1		152.9
	29 Under 75 mortality rate: cardiovascular	2012 - 14	292	71.8	75.7	135.0		39.3
	30 Under 75 mortality rate: cancer	2012 - 14	493	117.3	141.5	195.6		102.9
	31 Excess winter deaths	Aug 2011 - Jul 2014	157	15.3	15.6	31.0		2.3

Indicator notes

1 Index of Multiple Deprivation (IMD) 2015 2 % children (under 16) in low income families 3 Eligible homeless people not in priority need, crude rate per 1,000 households 4 5 A*-C including English & Maths, % pupils at end of key stage 4 resident in local authority 5 Recorded violence against the person crimes, crude rate per 1,000 population 6 Crude rate per 1,000 population aged 16-64 7 % of women who smoke at time of delivery 8 % of all mothers who breastfeed their babies in the first 48hrs after delivery 9 % school children in Year 6 (age 10-11) 10 Persons under 18 admitted to hospital due to alcohol-specific conditions, crude rate per 100,000 population 11 Under-18 conception rate per 1,000 females aged 15-17 (crude rate) 12 Current smokers, Annual Population Survey (APS) 13 % adults achieving at least 150 mins physical activity per week 14 % adults classified as overweight or obese, Active People Survey 15 Experimental statistics - % of cancers diagnosed at stage 1 or 2 16 Directly age sex standardised rate per 100,000 population 17 The number of admissions involving an alcohol-related primary diagnosis or an alcohol-related external cause (narrow definition), directly age standardised rate per 100,000 population 18 % people on GP registers with a recorded diagnosis of diabetes 19 Crude rate per 100,000 population 20 All new diagnoses (excluding Chlamydia under age 25), crude rate per 100,000 population 21 Directly age and sex standardised rate of emergency admissions, per 100,000 population aged 65 and over 22, 23 The average number of years a person would expect to live based on contemporary mortality rates 24 Rate of deaths in infants aged <1 year per 1,000 live births 25 Rate per 100,000 population 26 Directly age standardised mortality rate from suicide and injury of undetermined intent per 100,000 population (aged 10+) 27 Directly age standardised rate per 100,000 population 28 Directly age standardised rate per 100,000 population aged 35 and over 29 Directly age standardised rate per 100,000 population aged under 75 30 Directly age standardised rate per 100,000 population aged under 75 31 Ratio of excess winter deaths (observed winter deaths minus expected deaths based on non-winter deaths) to average non-winter deaths (three years)

† Indicator has had methodological changes so is not directly comparable with previously released values € "Regional" refers to the former government regions
# New indicator for Health Profiles 2016

More information is available at and Please send any enquiries to

You may re-use this information (not including logos) free of charge in any format or medium, under the terms of the Open Government Licence. To view this licence, visit

www.healthprofiles.info

Figure 18: Showing Health profile of Westminster. Source: (Public Health England, 2016).

SWOT ANALYSIS

Figure 15: Swot analysis matrix. Source: (Jurevicious, 2017).

According to Jurevicius, (2017) swot analysis has various ways of matrix in collecting information on external and internal issues which will have or result on impact in various organizations.

Below is a preparation of Swot analysis of strengths, weaknesses, opportunities and threats of the interventions evaluation.

SWOT ANALYSIS EVALUATION COMMUNITY ASSETS STRENGTHS AND WEAKNESS

Box 1:

Strengths	Weakness
• Food plays a great role in the socio-economic and cultural growth.	• Bioterrorism has a very low investment in research and evolution.
• Good reputation	• Lack of education awareness on illness prevention.
• Focus on population	• Margining demographics patterns of chronic illnesses.
• Great community network • Special expertise on Bioterrorism	• Public health problems in strong preparedness and response rate to the 21st century threats.
• Technology Advantages	• Lack of proper assessment for Bioterrorism agents.
	• Uncertain immune acknowledgement from the public insight.

Opportunities	Threats
• Worldwide consessor on developing vaccines on Ebola • Food is always on demand in Westminster and more in crisis predicaments. • Development of the proposed project for Bioterrorism. • Funding for the community • Health Promotions • Increase of various social network sites and health campaign.	• Lack of a disease surveillance on bioterrorism agents. • Funding • From biological agents. • Lack of co-ordination across the borough in tackling bioterrorism. • Change of Demographics • Economic slowing of issues.

Figure 16: Showing Swot Analysis Evaluation for Westminster City Council.

Public Health England, (2017) identified the health needs in Bioterrorism and developed a book on Anthrax as an urgent threat.

- Urgency A: Bioterrorism in Anthrax (BA)
- Urgency B: Measels (M)
- Urgency C: Food Poising (FP) E.Coli

Urgency A: BA

There have been few cases of anthrax in the UK on animals and heroin users in Scotland; mixing of heroin agents in contamination of anthrax spores that can be inhaled through smoking, injections or sniffed. Conversely, in England and Wales 30 cases were identified in the year 1981 and in 2015.

It is therefore stated that the threat is highly deadly to the environment establishing inhalation will cause higher level of mortality; one of the most Bioterrorism threats to the public is the use of Anthrax in the form of a biological weapon in large quantities by releasing numerous amount in spores using aerosol is a public health concern (Tidy, 2015). It is an illness of animals from goats, sheep, cattle, created by bacteria called Bacillus anthracis; the ailment is dangerous in humans because it leads to death in humans pertaining to B. anthracis this ailment can be passed on through various ways through contaminated animals substances by hair, hides, feces, and made up of ulcerative skin lesios (Rao, 2017).

Urgency A: BA Analysis

A hand book on Anthrax for England and wales in the year 2013 with an updated version for 2017 has been produced in the UK, called the "Green book" that stipulate guidelines on anthrax in Bioterrorism.

However, it has been confirmed by them that Anthrax can be treated completely with antibiotics if it has been ascertained at an early stage; and if it is left untreated, it will create infection leading to meningitis, toxemia, septicemia, and its deadly at 5% occurrences (Public Health England, 2017). Although there are guidelines on anthrax, there is more to be done in improving the preparedness of this deadly infection. For example, leaflets about Anthrax should be in every GP surgery and community hubs like libraries and housings hubs, so that the community can be aware of this biological weapon.

Urgency B: MEASSELS

According to the NHS, Choices (2017) measles is an ailment that is highly infectious and can lead to further complications such as pneumonia and encephalitis, but less common in the UK due to vaccination, it last for 7-10 days. However,

Westminster City Council (2016) draws attention to measles epidemic in the capital city imploring adolescence and parents to get vaccinated from MMR following the incidence; the present rate for vaccination in London is at 87%, 60 reported cases within a short period in two months and 48% of the outbreak involves adolescence age 15 and above. Below is a poster designed for a measel health campaign to be put in surgeries:

Figure 19: Showing a child with measels. Picture derived from (NHS Choices, 2017).

Urgency B: measels Analysis

These are the symptoms listed below with appearance at 10-14 days from the onset of infection. They are:

- High Temperature at 40c
- Feeling of discomfort
- High levels of Tiredness
- The loss of eating propely
- It affects Eyelids and it gets swollen
- Eye problems with watering feelings
- Grey white sports can be found in the mouth
- Throw up (Mayo Clinic, 2017).

Urgency C: FP

Food poising has its dangers and concerns and needs to be dealt with appropriately. NHS Choice, (2017) describes this ailment as consuming contaminated food, not so much of an issue as people feels better in a short period of time without treatment; it is therefore caused by some bacteria which are E-coli, salmonella, and norovirus which is a virus. The food safety team in West minister city council controls all food safety issues for businesses in premises and examines all occurrences of food poising; ensuring visits to ascertain that all foods are being used hygienically in a safe way to be eaten (Westminister City Council, 2017).

However, the Food Standard Agency (FSA) combined with the Advisory committee on Microbiological safety of Food (ACMSF) has suggests new regulations on all restaurants to cook their burgers and meat at 70 c cooked at the middle for approximately two minutes or 75 degrees for 30 seconds, to eliminate E. Coli (Jenkins, 2017).

Bellow is a poster campaign intervention on E.Coli:

Figure 20: Showing a poster on Rare burger campaign on E.Coli.

Urgency C: FP Analysis

It has been confirmed that there is no recorded food poising in Westminster council although concerns have been made for rare burger crackdown in the city of west End. Moreover, rare burgers have been found in certain places which raises E. coli food poising in the area (Prynn, 2012). This was supported by another incident that took place in the same year that lamb's liver should be taken off a menu at a restaurant in Westminster council precisely convent garden; it was reported that for liver to be served in a restaurant, it should be well cooked to meet the standards of the council (Davies, 2012).

Moreover, Westminster City Council (2017) has a team in food safety department that have produced guidelines in the following areas if you are going through food poising symptoms. They are listed below:

- Do not handle any food or prepare it in your job role.
- Stay away from work within 48 hours' time frame.
- It is advisable to drink lots of fluids and plenty of rest to gain better well-being.

- Stay away from preparation of food to other people.
- Think about sending a stool to your local GP for identification of food poising and help with food poising enquiry.

RECOMMENDATIONS

Leadership

One of the great attribute of Westminster council is their leadership skills in the vision for local individual and their representation; they have been set up by the London Healthcare devolution agreement that decides issues arising on important matters that affects daily wellbeing focusing on key interventions such as 'robust, transparent and equitable' keeping a close eye on budgets and services as one priority by shaping expenditures and focusing on key priorities for life in this strategy on spending's at a given time frame or over a certain period on what is needed through practice in service, learning, and delivery in different places (London Council, 2015).

However, leadership skills involve multidisciplinary team and network communication interventions. For example, contextual leadership skills must be followed where in the act of knowing when and how to lead in a situation and to possession the ability to follow and collaborate to achieve organisation goal.

The methodology adopted is determined by the context at various levels. The act of contextual leadership is the ability to understand an evolving environment, and having the capacity to capitalise on those evolving trends to achieve leadership objective.

Nonetheless, managing people during pre-attacks or definite bioterrorism issues should be well planned and collaborated with effective leadership skills and robust communication are vital (CDC,2017).

The significance of communication in Bioterrorism

Communication plays a pivotal role in the preparedness of emergency situations in Bioterrorism. According to Birnbach Success Solution, (2014) strategy implementation involves comprehensive communication through a crisis management group; by stressing the need of understanding certain strategies during and after the crisis. Moreover, communication in Bioterrorism needs a lot of effective collaboration in the community. Recognise all anthrax epidemics that arise within a short time frame which can be done in various ways such as surveillance, flights, and public input.

Community Resilience

Following an Anthrax attack, it is therefore advisable for the community to have strong resilience in adverse issues. Plough et al, (2013) defined the idea that community resilience is the maintaining of the community to stand firm in adversity and that it involves five areas which are psychological health, physical, economic, social and well-being.

However, all these areas listed should be dealt with holistically in emergency in health preparedness and introduce certain interventions to build community resilience. For example, Neighbourhood watch areas are helpful in building different strategies and activities.

PROJECT PROPOSAL

TITLE: "Saving lives" - Enhancing the response rate and the readiness of the public Health Sector to handle evolving Bioterrorism threat in Central London (Westminster).

Target Population: The overall population in Westminster

Proposal start date: December 2017

Proposal end date: December 2019

Proposal budget: 100,000

BACKGROUND

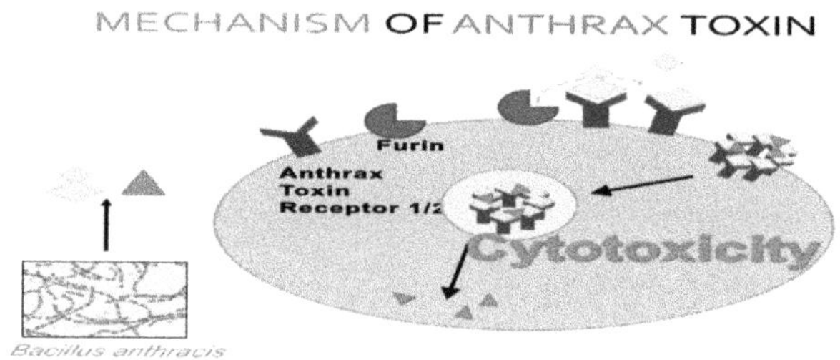

Figure 21: Showing the mechanism of anthrax toxin. Source, Slideplayer.com

Bioterrorism is a public health urgency in the UK, although there are growing terrorist threats in Central London and the UK as country. According to Pal et al; (2017) bioterrorism is used as a biological weapon and the outcome will be a large mortality cases which will create a big impact in public health, panics in the community and lots of social disturbances and thus readily needs quick response rate for public health preparedness.

Conversely, Pal et al; (2017) believes that there are various ways of passing on these biological agents, and can be released in the following ways:

- Body fluids and blood airways
- Inhalation through people around the area that goes through the respiratory system
- Contact by infected animals
- Oral -fecal passage in the form of objects, food intake, or contamination of infected person, through sexual activities.

ANTHRAX

CDC, (2015) defined Anthrax as a highly infectious illness from bacteria called Bacillus anthrax. It is a rare disease but can mainly occurs in association with infected animals, or product from poisonous animal products. Although it is common in places of agricultural areas as listed below:

- Caribbean
- Easter and Southern Europe
- Central and Southwestern Asia
- Sub-Saharan Africa

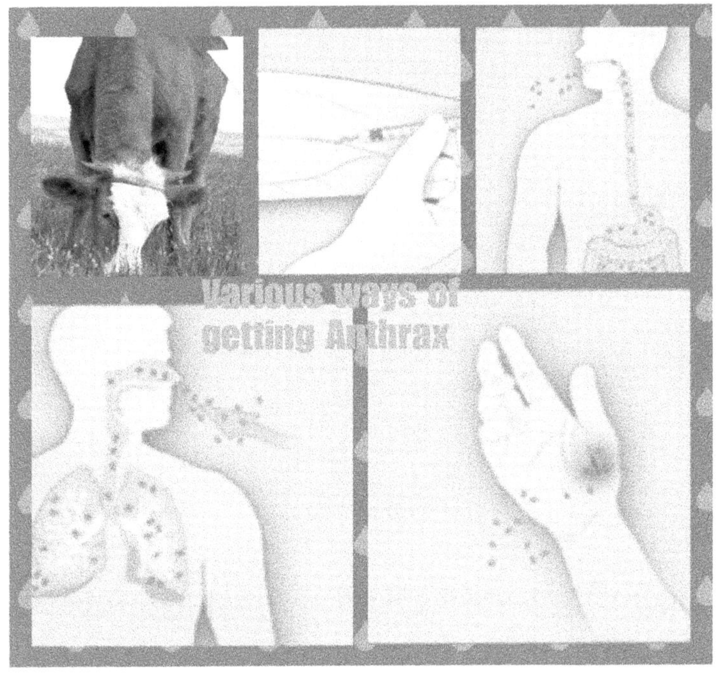

Figure 22: Showing the various ways of getting anthrax. Source: (CDC, 2017).

The various forms of anthrax are cutaneous anthrax, inhalation anthrax, Intestinal anthrax, and injection anthrax and the various uncommon things that that rarely occurs are person to person contact, airborne transmission from one person to the other (Tidy, 2015)

Bacillus Anthracis

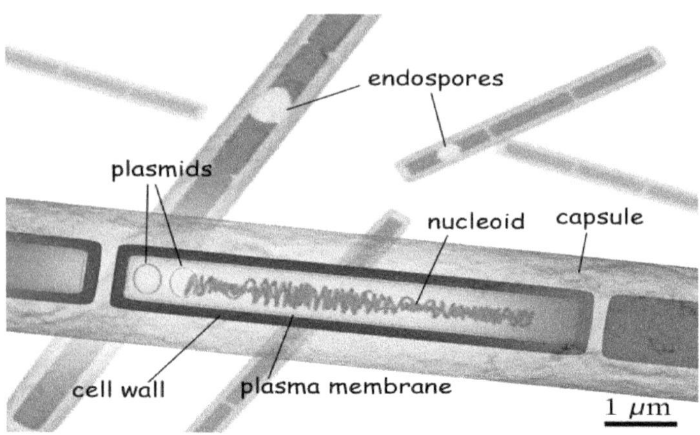

Figure 23: Showing Bacillus Anthracis. Source: CDC, 2017

This bacteria that create the disease Anthrax which is large in shape, rod shape and the living of this bacteria requires oxygen to breath freely; reproduction of this disease can occur in humans, soil, and animals. Bioterrorism has been associated with Bacillus anthracis in anthrax outbreak and does affect the community; globally, it was confirmed that there were only 100 cases which involves high mortality as it is deadly.

The breakthrough occurred in Scotland in the year 2009-2010 which was associated with heroin users (Dewar et al, 2015). CDC, (2017) listed three types of anthrax and how it affects people in the areas listed below:

Cutaneous Anthrax

It is reported that 95% of the deadly infection is from Cutaneous transmission from a cut or abrasion that occurs on the skin in the process of contaminated wool, hair products, leather, hides, of afflicted animals; approximately 20% of cases with the disease without treatment will cause death.

Inhalation Anthrax

This is a form of inhalation through breathing of the spores or bacteria and its associated with Bioterrorism as it is used as a biological weapon in a community. These are the few symptoms listed below very close symptoms linked with flu or cold.

In a form of mild fever
-Chills of cold
-Night time sweats
-Body muscle aches and pains.

This will later progress to different symptoms such as:
-High levels of breathing
-It affects the chest
-Creates tiredness.
-High levels of muscle pain
-Coughing
-Death can occur at a later stage

Gastrointestinal Anthrax

It's been confirmed that this type of anthrax generates in a hot climate and tropical areas such as Africa, Asia and Middle East. However, there have been no confirmed cases in the UK.

Below is a history of anthrax cases in England and wales.

Rationale

Anthrax is an epidemic disease that has a great impact -in humans especially in a country and a community, which is due to bioterrorist threats mainly on human population that creates high levels of mortality rates such as inhalation anthrax and cutaneous anthrax. Public Health England (2017) has produced a booklet called "Anthrax: The Green Book chapter 13", it provides guidelines on anthrax management against infectious illnesses.

According to Public Health England (2017) it has a long history in the UK from 1895 and humans are affected through the skin, very rarely on the breathing or gastro-intestinal tract. It states that presently, the chances of contacting continuous exposure on airborne anthrax spores is very limited as there are no industries in Great Britain that has the exposures. Below is Anthrax reported cases from 1981-2015 in England and Wales:

BOX 3:

Occupation (source of infection)	Number of cases
Slaughterman, butcher, fellmonger	5
Factory worker (imported wool)	1
Factory worker -/(bone meal fertilizer)	1
Factory worker (imported cotton, wool or leather	1
Labourer (leather bales)	1
Leather worker	1
Engineer (animal skins in Zambia)	1
Worked with horses	1
Builder	1
Farm worker	1
Animal hide drums	1
Injecting heroin use	11
Not identified	4

Figure 24: Showing Anthrax cases infection reported cases 1981-2015 in England and Wales. Source: (PHE, 2016).

Aims and Objective

The general goals of this proposal are:

Safeguarding of the community health care in Westminster city council.

Decreasing collisions of anthrax on Westminster city council community.

The main basis of this project is to improve on the readiness of the public health sector to handle evolving Bioterrorist threats on anthrax in Central London concentrating on the following objectives:

-Safeguarding the community in exposure to anthrax.

-Safeguarding the management team from exposure to anthrax (By means of vaccination).

-To improve people's knowledge of emergency interventions amongst Doctors, and Nurses, on antibiotics therapy procedures, policies, confidence, and competent.

-Identifying areas or limitations in procedures, plans, protocols, and delivering opportunities in resources for biological population casualty events.

-To provide Health Education training on anthrax as part of health promotion in emergency exercises in various hubs in the community (establish key information on resources e.g.: information leaflets, radio stations, postal boards, website information on anthrax).

-Improve understanding of people's roles, partners, and the role of the various incidents commanding system.

-Improve on behavioral change including perceptions on bioterrorism attacks or preparedness in the response rate (Medical model and behavioral change).
-To train hospital laboratory staff in preparedness to deal with chemical anthrax attacks samples.

-Improve support on social context in community resilience in Westminster city council and emotional behavioral support.

PLANNING

Figure 25: A picture of planning tool using SMART goals. Source: (Lamachenka, 2016).

Planning a project involves lots of collaborative practice with your team members. All staffing committee are chosen according to their various roles in terms of preparedness before and after anthrax attacks. To plan a project, a leader should use SMART goals which is specific, measurable accurate, realistic and timed. This is supported by Lamachenka, (2016) who established that a structure of SMART strategy should be specific, measurable, attainable, relevant and timed based; mainly because the organization can pay attention to decisions solely on these areas, as it enlightens a structure for goals and objectives using Gantt chart as a form of method in project planning is necessary.

All the listed task on the Gantt chart should be done as part of a team with designated member of different department of work. Some decisions can be done by the chief commanding Public Health Officer or according to specialize areas of expertise in Bioterrorism anthrax attacks.

All Health authorities involved in this project has a duty of care to safeguard the members of the public within their roles. However, health centers should be well informed and be ready for vaccination across the community. The chief public health officer with other team members and Health consultants will give advice to the community in prevention and response issues information booklets on Bio safety measures.

The National Health Services and Public Health England department plays a pivotal role in emergency difficulties because they are the main body to help the population in the community.Here are twelve areas below as an example of various schedule mission using a Gantt chart.

RE-AIM FRAMEWORK

Initially, “RE-AIM” framework has been used to established framework for unchanging outlying of research and later to arrange reviews and documentations on illnesses management and health promotion in various places. Here are different types used in the "RE-AIM" framework, Reach, Effectiveness, Adoption, implementation, and management. This is an effective way in doing a project, as

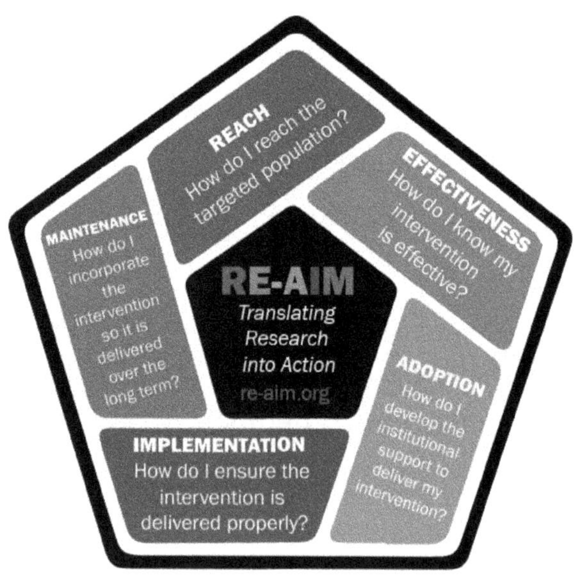

FIGURE 26: Showing the framework on RE-AIM. Source, (Cummings Online Resources, 2017).

REACH

Currently, there are 48% of female and 52% of male population in Westminster City Council (ONS,2017). Radio king online which is a popular radio station in Westminster that is accessed by both young and old; it has over 40,000 listeners every month (Westminster City Council, 2017).

Radio stations are effective ways to send messages across quickly and accurately, as people are quite busy to read things, however, by listening to the radio, the message will be sent fast, and can be reach to the community within a short period of time (See appendix 2 for health Promotion and education)

EFFECTIVENESS

Anthrax effectiveness interventions in the UK has been good in terms of policies and procedures but not effective in terms of preparedness to the public. The entire population should be well informed in different ways to make safety precautions in Bioterrorist anthrax by effective schemes catered for the community. People in the community are not knowledgeable in areas of safety issues on the contrary subject, therefore

ADOPTION

The chief head officer in Bioterrorism in Westminster, would join hands with his team members and looked at surveillance areas and populations and splits the teams into their various roles and Safeguarding members of the organization (appendix 1 on the Gantt chart) Safeguarding members by making sure all team members are vaccinated and cover all safety precautions.

IMPLEMENTATION: BOX 3

This project will involve skilled health professionals who are specialized in anthrax Bioterrorism attacks including health professionals. Public health professionals are therefore designated in their various roles.

Activity	Year 1	Year 2	Year 3
Community education	4 staffs	3 staffs	3 staffs
Radio stations	2	1	1
Poster campaign	3	3	2
Design Leaflets	3	3	2
Safety of equipments training	5	5	4
Staff Roles	4	3	3
Reporting of information	4	3	3

RESOURCE PLAN. BOX :4

Main Activity	Volume	period	Total
Staff/Survellance	20	3 years	60
Education	4	3 years	12
Health Promotion	4	3 years	12
Training	2	3 years	6
vaccination	18	3 years	24
Social Support	16	3 years	48
Emmergency management	12	2 years	24

The implementation plan is projected over a period of 3 years with a minimum of 20 working staff mainly from three main focus point:

- Education
- Implementation
- Training

The Resources would be strategically allocated by the senior management team that would design the implementation plan focusing on education campaign, training of staff and ensuring resilience to handle emergency.

The Figure 25 illustrate the 12 months plan and how the project would be managed across the timeline with senior management, training and review which would be ongoing.

MAINTENANCE

Maintaining this project will focus on areas of behavioural change and linking it with the health model. Appropriate education tool would be distributed to the farmer to know and report early signs of anthrax with protocols on the disposal of animals.

MONITORING AND EVALUATION

Prepardness of public health concern standards has been done in order to support the planning strategy. Conversly, if ever a bioterriorist threat does happen, Public Health England and the government will monitor the problems effectively.

SUSTAINABILITY OF THE LIFE LONG OF THE PROJECT

This project needs to be assessed and planned for ongoing process.

COSTING. BOX:4

Cost Allocation strategy for prevention in anthrax attack

cost	Volume	Unit cost	Total Annual

			cost
Staff	20	variable	40,000
vaccination	5,000	1	5,000
Educational Campaign	200,000 plus population	-	10,000
Health Material	40,000	0.1	2,000
Training	20	200	4,000
Emergency Staff	18	1	14,000
Administrative Cost	-	-	6,000
Cash Flow			6,000
Total			100,000

REFLECTION

Stefano et al, (2014) pointed out that reflection in learning experiences create productive, stronger confidence in your goals in self worth and this can be a transitionasl phase into huge way of learning main lessons taught by grace experiences. I have gained an insight in bioterrorism and more over Westminister City Council , and have learned so much in putting this proposal, and its vital to establish positive and negative output for a better understanding in the near future.

The detail investigations in public public health will continue in surveillance on population. I have examined the preparedness of Bioterrorism on anthrax attacks in various levels from the community and in health.

What was interesting on this project was the various interventions and the prevalence of the diseases, and how it will affect the population. It is vital for education to be available at a mass level to health staff, veterinary, and other health proffesionals when anthrax cases are diagnosed and few progression analysis and to correct any mistakes in the future.

What I will do differently is to take on board all risk assessment and implement it better.

REFERENCE

Australian Government Department of Health 2015. PH Commissioning. Department of Health Initiative an Australian Government Needs assessment guide. [Online] Available at:<https://www.health.gov.au/internet/main/publishing.nsf/Content/98D184E26BF30004CA257F9A000718F4/$File/PHN%20Needs%20Assessment%20Guide.pdf> [Accessed 3rd December 2017]

Barrasa, Greubb, 2014. History of biological warfare and bioterrorism. [Online] Available at:<https://www.sciencedirect.com/science/article/pii/S1198743X14641744> [Pdf] https://doi.org/10.1111/1469-0691.12706

[Accessed 4th November 2017].

Baggott A., 2011. Public Health Policy &Politics. 2nd ed. New York: Palgrave Macmillan.

Birnbach Success Solution 2014. The importance of Communication in emergency preparedness plans [Online] Available at:<http://birnbachsuccesssolutions.com/hr-consulting/the-importance-of-communication-in-emergency-preparedness-plans/> [Accessed 10th November 2017].

Cara L. Pennel, Kenneth R. McLeroy, James N. Burdine, Matarrita-Cascante, D., Wang J., 2016. Community Health Needs Assessment: Potential for Population Health Improvement [pdf] Available at:

http://online.liebertpub.com/doi/pdf/10.1089/pop.2015.0075?download=true& > [Accessed 1st November 2017].

CDC, 2017. CDC and Bioterrorism Response. Bioterrorism Readiness Plan: A Template for Healthcare Facilities. [Online] Available from:

<https://www.scribd.com/document/243991883/CDC-and-Bioterrorism-Response> [Accessed 2nd December 2017].

Cummings Online Resources 2017. RE-AIM: Introduction [Online] Available at:<http://azhin.org/cummings/re-aim> [Accessed 3rd December 2017].

Dahlgren G., Whitehead M., 1991. Policies and Strategies to Promote Social Equity in Health. Stocholm, Sweden: Institute for Futures Studies.

Davies C., 2012. Raymond Blanc ordered to take lamb's liver off menu after food poisoning [Online] Available at: < https://www.theguardian.com/lifeandstyle/2012/nov/13/raymond-blanc-lambs-liver-food-poisoning> [Accessed 2nd December 2017].

Dearden, 2017. UK security services preparing to launch new crackdown on terrorism as Isis attack threat rises. [Online] Available from: <http://www.independent.co.uk/news/uk/home-news/uk-terror-attacks-isis-threat-rising-new-terrorism-strategy-propaganda-online-islamic-state-a8072641.html?amp> [Accessed 30th November 2017].

Farmer B.,2017. Bioterrorism could kill more than nuclear War, Bill Gates to warn world leaders [Online] Available at:http://www.telegraph.co.uk/news/2017/02/17/biological-terrorism-could-kill-people-nuclear-attacks-bill/ [Accessed 2nd November 2017.

Healthier Northwest London 2016. "How do we think about outcomes holistically" [Online] Available at:<http://integration.healthiernorthwestlondon.nhs.uk/section/how-do-we-think-about-

outcomes-holistically-> [Accessed 12th November 2017].

Jenkins, L., 2017. New regulations on cooking burgers come into Force [online] Available at:< https://www.thecaterer.com/articles/497150/new-regulations-on-cooking-burgers-come-into-force> [Accessed 2 December 2017].

Joint Strategic Needs Assessment. (2016, June 24). Physical activity: a needs assessment for Hammersmith and Fulham, Kensington and Chelsea, and Westminster. [Online] Available at JSNA: <http://www.jsna.info/sites/default/files/Triborough%20Physical%20Activity%20JSNA.pdf> [Accessed 20th November 2017].

Joint Strategic Health Needs Assessment for Westminster 2017/2020 [Pdf] Available at:http://transact.westminster.gov.uk/docstores/publications_store/consultations/joint_health _wellbeing_strategy.pdf [Accessed 4th November 2017].

Jurevicius, 2013. Swot Analysis - Do It Properly! [online] Available at: <https://www.strategicmanagementinsight.com/tools/swot-analysis-how-to-do-it.html> [Accessed 1st December 2017].

Lamachenka, A., 2016. Capterra Project Management Blog. 10 SMART Goal Setting Best Practices for Project Planning [Online] Available at:<https: blog.capterra.com/10-smart-goal-setting-best-practices-for-project-planning/> [Accessed 1st December 2017].

London Medicine and Health Care 2017. London's NHS Infrastructure. [Online]Available at:<https://www.londonmedicine.ac.uk/fam londons-landscape/national-health-service/london-s-nhs-infrastructure/ > [Accessed 11th November].

Nsubuga J., 2017.Met Police have prevented seven terror attacks in London since March. [Online] Available at: http://metro.co.uk/2017/09/24/met-police-have-prevented-seven-terror-attacks-in-london-since-march-6952650/ > [Accessed 11th November 2017].

MEDTV 2017. [Online] Available at:<http://anthrax.emedtv.com/gastrointestinal-anthrax/gastrointestinal-anthrax.html> [Accessed 10th November].

NHS Choices 2017. Food Poisoning [Online] Available at:<https://www.nhs.uk/conditions/food-poisoning/> [Accessed 30th November 2017].

NHS CHOICES 2017. Measles [Online] Available at:<https://www.nhs.uk/conditions/measles/> [Accessed 12th November 2017].

NHS Central London Clinical Commissioning Group 2017. About Us [Online] Available at:<http://www.centrallondonccg.nhs.uk/about-us.aspx> [Accessed 2nd November 2017].

ONS MYE 2014. Subnational population projections for England:2014based projections [Online] Available at<https://www.ons.gov.uk/peoplepopulationandcommunity/populationandmigration/populationprojections/bulletins/subnationalpopulationprojectionsforengland/2014basedprojections> [Accessed 1st December].

ONS 2017. Population and migration [Online] Available at <https://www.ons.gov.uk/peoplepopulationandcommunity/populationandmigration> [Accessed 2nd December 2017].

ONS, 2014. Subnational population projections for England: 2014-based projections. [Online] Available at:<https://www.ons.gov.uk/peoplepopulationandcommunity/populationandmigration/populationprojections/bulletins/subnationalpopulationprojectionsforengland/2014basedprojections> [Accessed 10th November 2017].

Pal M., Tsegaye M., Girzaw F., Bedada H., Godishala V., Kandi V., 2017. An Overview on Biological Weapons and Bioterrorism. American Journal of Biomedical Research, [e-journal]5(2) pp.24-34. http//dx.doi.org/10.12691/ajbr-5-2-2.

Prynn J., 2012. No food poisoning cases recorded but Westminster council presses on with rare burger crackdown [Online] Available at: <https:// www.standard.co.uk/news/london/no-food-poisoning-cases-recorded-but-westminster-council-presses-on-with-rare-burger-

crackdown-8412718.html> [Accessed 1st December 2017].

Public Health England 2016. Westminster Health Profile [Online] Available at:< www.healthprofiles.info> [Accessed 20th November 2017].

Public Health England, 2017. Westminster Health Profile [Online] Available at :<http://psnc.org.uk/kensington-chelsea-and-westminster-lpc/wp-content/uploads/sites/73/2017/05/2016-1.pdf> [Accessed 13th November 2017].

Public Health England, 2017.Anthrax Green Book. Chapter 13. [Online] Available at:<https://www.gov.uk/government/uploads/system/uploads/attachment_data/file/593305/Green_Book_Chapter_13.pdf> [pdf] [Accessed 1st December 2017].

Rao T.V., 2017. Anthrax [Online] Available at:<https://www.slideshare.net/mobile/doctorrao/anthrax-teaching> [Accessed 11th November 2017].

Rowe, A., McClelland, A., Billingham, K. Community Health Needs Assessment. An introductory guide for the family Mental health nurse in Europe Part 1: A pack for practitioners Part 2: A pack for trainers [Online] Available at:<www.populationhttp://www.euro.who.int/__data/assets/pdf_file/0018/102249/E73494.pdf> [Accessed 10th November 2017].

St. Mungo's Broadway. (2015/16). Combined Homelessness and Information Network [Online] Available at:< http://data.london.gov.uk/dataset/chain-reports/resource/6c740944-3816-4f21-bbcf-04505b59c76b> [Accessed 5th December 2017].

Stefano G. D., Gino, F., Pisano, G., Staats, B., 2014. Learning by Thinking: How Reflection Improves Performance [Online] Available at :<https://hbswk.hbs.edu/item/learning-by-thinking-how-reflection-improves-performance>

Verisure 2017. Crime Statistics for Westminster. [Online] Available at:

<https://www.verisure.co.uk/advice-and-help/crime-statistics/westminster-crime-rates> [Accessed 10th November 2017].

Westminster City Council 2016. City of Westminster Economic Baseline Report (LEA) [Online] Available at: http://www.onewestminster.org.uk/files/onewestminster/city_of_westminster_economic_report_january_2016_01.pdf

Westminster City Council. (2015). Primary Care Modelling. Westminster City Council Health and

Wellbeing Board. [Online] Available at: <http://committees.westminster.gov.uk/documents/s16609/8%20-%20appendix%20for%20Primary%20Care%20needs%20modelling.pdf

Westminster City Council 2014. Westminster Profile [Online] Available at:<http://transact.westminster.gov.uk/docstores/publications_store/research/westminster_profile%202014.pdf> [Accessed 11th November 2017]

Westminster City Council 2017. Westminster Population [Online] Available

at:<https://www.westminster.gov.uk/westminster-population> [Accessed 12th November 2017].

Westminster City Council 2014. Economic Report LEA Baseline Study Version II, Westminster City Council (Intelligence and

Analysis Team/ City Planning Delivery Unit). Local Economic Assessment Westminster [pdf] Available at<:http://transact.westminster.gov.uk/docstores/publications_store/LEA_V.II_November2014_FINAL.pdf>

Westminster City Council 2017.Health and Wellbeing Strategy for Westminster 2017-2022 [pdf] Available at:<http://committees.westminster.gov.uk/documents/s20651/Appendix%201%20Health%20and%20Wellbeing%20Strategy%20for%20Westminster.pdf> [Accessed 20th November 2017].

Westminster City Council 2017. Your MP'S. [Online] Available at:http://committees.westminster.gov.uk/mgMemberIndexMP.aspx?bcr=1 > [Accessed 2nd December 2017].

Westminster City council 2017. Joint Strategic Needs Assessment. [Online] Available at :<https://www.westminster.gov.uk/jsna-joint-strategic-needs-assessment-health-wellbeing> [Accessed de 3rd November 2017].

Westminster City council 2017. Your MPs. MP's Westminster City Council [Online] Available at:<http://committees.westminster.gov.uk/mgMemberIndexMP.aspx?bcr=1> [Accessed 6th November 2017].

Westminster City Council 2017. Westminster City Council Population [Online]

<https://www.westminster.gov.uk/Westminster-population> [Accessed 12th November 2017].

Westminster City Council 2017. Social care. [Online] Available at:<https://www.westminster.gov.uk/social-care> [Accessed 10th November 2017].

Westminster City Council 2016. Economic Report LEA Baseline Study [Online] Available at:<http://www.onewestminster.org.uk/files/onewestminster/city_of_westminster_economic_report_january_2016_01.pdf> [Accessed 1st November 2017]

Westminster City Council 2017. Health and well-being board [Online] <https://www.westminster.gov.uk/health-and-wellbeing-board> [Accessed 7th November 2017].

Westminster City Council 2014. WESTMINSTER'S ECONOMY DEVELOPING WESTMINSTER'S CITY PLAN [Online] Available at:<http://transact.westminster.gov.uk/docstores/publications_store/westminster's%20econo

my%20CM%20Version1.pdf> [Accessed 9th November 2017].

Swat analysis image. [online] Available at:<https://www.shutterstock.com/image-illustration/bioterrorism-word-cloud-464491466 > [Accessed 10th November 2017].

Westminster City Council 2017. Report a food safety concern [Online] Available at:<https://www.westminster.gov.uk/report-food-safety-concern> [Accessed 1st December 2017].

Westminster City Council 2017. Food Safety for businesses [Online] Available at:<https://www.westminster.gov.uk/food-safety-businesses> [Accessed 30th November 2017].

Westminster City Council 2016. London measles outbreak raises public Health Concern [Online] Available at: <https://www.westminster.gov.uk/london-measles-outbreak> [Accessed 29th November 2017].

Your B-School partner 2017. Using your business school to enhance both Technology Transfer Office and Educational Activities [Online] Available at:<http://player.slideplayer.com/19/5776518/# [Accessed 10th November 2017].

www.ingramcontent.com/pod-product-compliance
Ingram Content Group UK Ltd.
Pitfield, Milton Keynes, MK11 3LW, UK
UKHW020239250726
13967UKWH00001B/448

9 780244 774769